TIME TO TALK

TIME TO TALK

An Exclusive Interview with Fethullah Gülen

Ekrem Dumanlı

BLUE DOME

New York

Published by Blue Dome Press
244 5th Avenue, Suite D-149
New York, NY 10001, USA

www.bluedomepress.com

Editor: Özgür Küçük

Library of Congress Cataloging-in-Publication Data
Gülen, Fethullah.
[Konusma zamani. English]
Time to talk : an exclusive interview with Fethullah Gülen / Ekrem
Dumanli.
pages cm
ISBN 978-1-935295-61-7 (alk. paper)
1. Gülen, Fethullah--Interviews. 2. Turkey--Politics and government.
3. Muslim scholars--Interviews. I. Dumanli, Ekrem, 1964- II. Title.
BP80.G8A5 2015
297.092--dc23
2014040109

ISBN: 978-1-935295-61-7

Printed by
Imak Ofset, Istanbul - Turkey

Contents

Introduction

What could an opinion leader do against grave accusations, ungrounded lies and slanderous remarks by a politician? Of course the logical thing to do is to respond to these accusations and lies and to offer what is true vis-à-vis the lies and slanders. It is not possible to believe that he would resort to any means other than a civilian initiative and a verbal defense.

Turkey was shaken by a huge corruption investigation on Dec. 17, 2013. The investigation involving the son of Recep Tayyip Erdoğan, who prime minister at the time, as well as four ministers in his Cabinet led to the removal of the four ministers. Instead of launching a campaign to address this state of corruption, the government staged a counterattack to create an enemy and implement the "parallel state" tactic it had been devising for a long time. Moves to spread disinformation that were started as part of as well this plan are still being made through the misdirection and manipulation of the critical state institutions as the media outlets controlled by the government.

Fethullah Gülen, who had remained silent during the period between Dec. 17 and March 30, 2014, opted to offer humble responses to the grave accusations, lies and slander directed at himself and the Hizmet Movement. He never consented to the rupture of the ties of brotherhood between the people, the destruction of the environment of peace, and the escalation of tension vis-à-vis this polarizing language as well as efforts to spread disinformation that sought to trigger trouble along Turkey's fault lines.

As you read the interview, you will see that Gülen, the representative of the Hizmet Movement, which has been engaged in educational activities on a voluntary basis in a number of countries around the world, upholds that there is no retreat from democracy, and that those who had been trying to stifle the corruption investigations that became public on Dec. 17 by relying on state institutions and power will be eventually brought to justice.

Time to Talk is also a defense manifesto of the Hizmet Movement which has been engaged in educational activities around the world and in Turkey for five decades. The content of the talk once again confirms that the Movement, which has never been involved in any illegal activity whatsoever since its inception, expects nothing but the establishment of bridges of peace and brotherhood throughout the world.

I now leave you with Gülen's responses to the questions on the association of the Hizmet Movement with the so-called "parallel state," the Dec. 17 corruption investigation and many other critical inquiries.

Part 1

_____

We have always been in favor of the law and universal values. We will remain the same. The law should be respected even in critical times when you are subjected to grave assaults.

No one has ever used such expressions before

Y ou have in recent times been the target of all sorts of preposterous lies and slander. Very strong words have been used. But despite these accusations, you have remained silent, refraining from giving a response.

I have of course been very saddened. What evidence are they relying on when speaking so confidently? I really don't know. I don't know of any historical incident in which an unbeliever (hostile to Islam) had ever uttered a similar word or accusation against those who believe (i.e., Muslims). I did not expect it from those who uttered them. I do not want to say that they are lying. Rather, I prefer to say that they are misleading the people with incorrect statements. For the time being, I find consolation in the fact that, throughout history, but particularly during times of discord (*fitna*), we can see that people were defamed and the believers denigrated, and people who did not know the truth about the development were implicated in that sin. So who are we, then? People even hurled accusations at Aisha, the Mother of the Believers, in the Age of Happiness (i.e., when Prophet Muhammad, peace and blessings be upon him, was alive). Even worse, unbelievers cast aspersions on God. The Qur'an frequently refers to these aspersions. "God has taken unto Himself a son," they say. Or "The angels are the daughters of God," they say. These inappropriate and improper descriptions about God always bother me. God, the prophets and the saints were all subjected to this improper treatment. And today, some believers do the same to an ordinary, worthless person who is me. This is not a big thing, I conclude, and I find consolation in this fact.

Everyone acts in accordance with their character. People capable of oppression engage in oppression. But because you have no teeth, you cannot bite anyone. And it's better that way. Let them indulge in oppression. Let them go on with oppression. And let us be guided with poise and vigilance and ask for God's mercy and forgiveness for those who have the capacity to turn back from their errors, and let us ask God to save them. Being on the receiving end of slander, aspersions and conspiracies has and always will be the destiny of those traveling on this path. However, prudence and foresight undo such adversity. No conspiracy or slander can resist prudence. Those who let themselves be driven by these conspiracies and illusions should try to revise their path in the light of the Qur'an and the Sunnah (i.e., the example of the Prophet).

Ten times the oppression seen during the Feb. 28 coup

You are one of the main victims of the Feb. 28, 1997 postmodern coup. A lawsuit was brought against you as a result of an unprecedented media lynch campaign and this lawsuit dragged on for eight years. A group of people who see hostility against you as their raison d'être now claim that you supported the Feb. 28 coup, and by

*doing so they try to pave the way to further victimiza-
tion. Do you feel like you are re-living the same events?*

We have gone through these kinds of things many times. I was sentenced to six-and-a-half months in prison on the charge of "penetrating into the state apparatus" at the time of the March 12, 1971 military memorandum. At that time, Article 163 (of the Turkish Penal Code (TCK)) stood as a guillotine for Muslims until it was abolished by (former Prime Minister Turgut) Özal. In the wake of the Sept. 12, 1980 military coup, the authorities tracked me for six years as if I were a criminal. Raids were carried out. Our friends were harassed. In a sense, it became a sort of lifestyle for us to live under constant surveillance in a coup atmosphere. What we are seeing today is 10 times worse than what we saw during the military coups.

But despite everything, I don't complain. This time, we face similar treatment but at the hands of civilians who we think follow the same faith as us. I should acknowledge that this inflicts extra pain on us. All we can do is say "This, too, shall pass," and remain patient.

I worked hard to prevent the anti-democratic events of Feb. 28

Mention is made about your criticisms concerning Necmettin Erbakan, who served as prime minister at the time of the Feb. 28, 1997 coup. You are claimed to have supported that coup.

Everyone knew and saw that the Turkish Armed Forces (TSK) grew uneasy when the Welfare Party (RP) came in first in the elections. Clouds were gathering, but had not yet turned into a storm. I remember (journalists) the late Yavuz Gökmen, Fehmi Koru and Fatih Çekirge from Ankara. I shared my thoughts and feelings with them. I received unfair and unfitting reactions. Yet there were also others who had realized the imminent danger.

When, riding on the wave of social reactions amassing in the wake of the Susurluk scandal, certain groups implemented the coup, it was too late. My name was added to the report prepared by the National Intelligence Organization (MİT) about the Susurluk scandal (the 1996 Susurluk affair exposed links between the Turkish state, the criminal underworld and Turkish security forces) at the last moment. Although I later learned who did this, I never held any suspicions about believers (i.e., pious Muslims). Then came the Feb. 28 coup. The second article of the infamous statement demanded that our schools be nationalized in accordance with the Law on the Unification of Education. Tension was building and everyone was searching for ways to save the country from this predicament with minimal damage. And like many others, I said early elections might be the cure. I suggested early elections should be held under a new election law. This was not an idea voiced only by me, but also by many others, most notably Korkut Özal. There were even some pro-government groups and media outlets that thought the same and ran headlines to that effect. A brief look through the archives will reveal who said and wrote what.

There is another aspect. I explained to the then-Labor Minister Necati Çelik the coup atmosphere that was forming in the country at the time. Several witnessed this conversation. Alaattin Kaya (the former owner of the *Zaman* daily) and Melih Nural (a member of the Board of Trustees of Turgut Özal University) were with us during that meeting. "They are planning to get rid of the government," said. I worked hard to avert any anti-democratic development. Minister Çelik enthusiastically listened to my worries, and then left. He conveyed my concerns to Erbakan. However, Erbakan did not opt to take measures to prevent adverse developments.

Likewise, I tried to explain the impending threat to (former Prime Minister) Tansu Çiller, briefing her about the negative developments. "Let us act with moderation," Çiller responded. And this saddened me. I did not venture into details. Having realized that I could not explain the danger to anyone, I was urged to say something to avert an incident that would lead to a possible coup, examples of which we already witnessed in this region.

Early elections could have defeated the plots

I am in no position to tell anyone, "You have failed." Everyone knows that I show due respect to the people entitled to represent the nation. At that time, making mention of Abu Bakr (the first caliph) and 'Umar ibn Abd al-Aziz (an Umayyad caliph known for his righteousness), I asserted that it would not be a regression for the government to resign from office. If a mass resignation of deputies from Parliament—which would trigger a process leading to early elections—would avert more serious disasters, it should be employed—which also applies to the coups of May 27, 1960 and Sept. 12, 1980. Indeed, in response to the e-memorandum of April 27, 2007, the ruling Justice and Development Party (AK Party) decided to hold early elections and was thereby able to avert disaster. The tactics employed with this memorandum were similar to those wielded by anti-democratic forces during the Feb. 28 process, and the early elections card really worked. Thus, my message was: "Amend the election law and hold early elections."

I should note that a closer look at the Susurluk report and the memorandum of Feb. 28 reveals that the Hizmet Movement was one of the main targets of the junta. What happened later was the implementation of that intention. Any claim to the contrary would be unfair and misguided.

Scapegoating Hizmet became a pattern

In our previous meetings, you had stated, referring to the claim that the Hizmet Movement is trying to take Fenerbahçe under its control, that it is absurd to make such a claim. What would you like to say about this claim in light of the latest information that has emerged?

Yes. Fenerbahçe is an outstanding sports club. As far as I see, its management, audience and fans tend to act in unison. This solidarity is the envy of many. And who should be disturbed by this? When Galatasaray saw success in the European championships, I rejoiced over its achievements. It is my hope that Beşiktaş, Trabzonspor and the country's other teams are very successful. They should make their mark in the world. From this perspective, with which apolitical goals can you explain efforts to bring Fenerbahçe or any other club under control? The emerging trend of our time is to attribute every inexplicable event to the Hizmet Movement and use it as a scapegoat. It has been understood that this claim (the Hizmet Movement taking over Fenerbahçe) has turned out to be an aspersion.

Gov't adopts double standards in court cases

A large number of suspects were released in legal cases and investigations that were closely followed by the people, Ergenekon being the prime example. How do you assess this matter?

We will side with what the laws dictate and specify. The remark that a plot was staged against the army was a trick. They attempted to blame the movement for what they actually did. They convened Parliament to make a law for a single person. They could have acted with the same sensitivity with respect to these people as well. A release is one thing; a trial is another. They are still being tried. The legal decision should be respected. We have always been in favor of the law and universal values. We will remain the same. The law should be respected even in critical times when you are subjected to grave assaults.

Part 2

I have been preaching for about 60 years. I have always said the same thing. Let this be my legacy. Let my brothers and sisters who have sympathy for me—though I do not deserve it—distance themselves miles away from such corrupt practices and let them not turn a blind eye to such practices.

Neither the *Mecelle* nor demagogy can explain the theft of public property

A certain section of the media has claimed that the graft and bribery investigations were masterminded by the Hizmet Movement. How do you assess the current state of this matter?

Some people and groups persistently continue to hurl unfounded accusations at the Hizmet Movement although we have issued numerous denials, explanations and corrections. As I have noted previously, some prosecutors and judicial police serving under them performed the duties required of them by law, but they apparently did not know that it was a crime to hunt down criminals! In other words, these people did not expect that they would be victimized for performing their duties. A columnist—I think it was Yavuz Semerci—recently wrote, "One day, these people will be decorated with medals." Unfortunately, the officials who conducted the Dec. 17 probe and thousands of officials who had nothing to do with the probe were sent into exile and reassigned. They were victimized and the rights of their families were violated. And then, as if nothing had happened, some people started to accuse the Hizmet Movement. And they told lies one after another. They continue to do so.

First of all, these graft and bribery investigations were not novel. Eight to nine months ago, the country's intelligence service reported that a person, who might be a spy for Iran, had established close ties with ministers, their sons and even the Cabinet. This report was ignored. Then this development was reported extensively in the media, particularly in the papers close to the government. No attention was paid then either. The government did not take measures against corruption. But when the police operations were launched on Dec. 17 as part of the graft investigation, they apparently thought they could get away by hurling accusations against certain people or groups.

I have said this before. I have no connection to those who organized these operations. I have repeatedly stated that I do not know any of them, but they continue to claim that those prosecutors and police officers are linked to me.

What disappointed me was the position adopted by certain politicians who I thought to be dignified and honest people. It was my expectation that these people—whom I have known for a long time and who I believe would not go against their conscience and uprightness—would not keep silent in the face of corrupt practices and bribery. Or so I thought. I expected them to show the same reaction as, say, Özal would exhibit in the face of such illegal affairs. But they did not. Because they remained silent, others found the courage to proceed with their destructive plans. They did what had never been done in the history of the Turkish Republic. Turkey launched a crackdown on those who investigated the corruption instead of on those who engaged in corrupt practices.

Islam's sanctions on this matter are clear. There are moral principles that prohibit corruption. There are even punishments for certain acts. No act of corruption can be approved of. No corruption can be left unpunished. From a moral point of view, it should be noted that if sins or errors remain restricted to the individual sphere and they do not affect the society, then Islam preaches that those individuals should be forgiven. Islam does not permit the dignity and honor of those sinners to be damaged. These two points should not be confused with each other. In other words, when the rights of other people are breached during the committal of those sins, Islam urges us to be extremely sensitive. For instance, 'Umar ibn al-Khattab (the second caliph) removed Iyaz ibn al-Ghanam. He removed the governor, the regional governor, the governor of Africa and Amr ibn al-'As from office.

How can I say something that would destroy my life in the Hereafter?

Likewise, he removed from office another famous governor, the conqueror who fought in the Battle of al-Qadisiya against the Persians, and recalled him to Medina. This governor was in fact not guilty, as there were only rumors about him. 'Umar concluded that if there are rumors or allegations about him, this means he has lost prestige and could no longer act as governor. 'Umar even removed Khalid ibn al-Walid from office on the suspicion that he might be involved in corruption. At that time, the Battle of Yarmuk was under way. Don't think ill of Khalid ibn al-Walid. This magnificent commander had only a horse and a sword when he died. He was a very great commander, God-fearing and pious. In other words, 'Umar did not turn a blind eye to allegations of corruption. He closely investigated the matter.

If there are acts of bribery, theft, clientelism, bid rigging, etc., which run contrary to the interests of the nation, and if these acts are covered up, God will hold us accountable for them. But it appears that some people nurtured certain expectations... If among those who conducted the graft investigations were some people who might be connected to the Hizmet Movement, was I supposed to tell these people, "Turn a blind eye to the corruption charges"? It appears to me that some people were expecting me to do this. Did they expect me to do this? How can I say something that would ruin my afterlife? How else can I act?

This is a point I had previously made. If the people who were accused of being members of a "parallel network" within the state had been in breach of laws or regulations, why haven't they been punished yet? I heard tens of thousands of public servants were reshuffled or sent into exile, but I heard no investigation launched into any act of misconduct or breach of laws or regulations at those institutions. Did you hear of any?

I have been preaching for about 60 years. I have always said the same thing. Let this be my legacy. Let my brothers and sisters who have sympathy for me-though I do not deserve it—distance themselves miles away from such corrupt practices and let them not turn a blind eye to such practices. Let them do whatever they are supposed to under the law. The Qur'an refers to such corrupt practices as "ghulul." Ghulul means taking something to which one is not entitled, or benefiting from it in an unfair manner, or stealing something from public funds, or betraying a trust. Thus, abuse of public goods or funds constitutes such a sin. This may be in the form of several cents or dollars or bags full of money. It may be in the form of acquiring a public position without merit or capacity. Any opportunity a person benefits from although they do not deserve it is considered ghulul.

Neither the *Mecelle* nor demagogy can be used to explain stealing what belongs to the public

The most tragic part is that, by committing ghulul, one unknowingly damages the very foundations of his or her religious beliefs. When we start to act in a dishonest manner in our personal life, we unknowingly damage how others think, understand and view religion. I think people who are attracted to political posts and positions tend to employ these "spoils" and commissions. In the final analysis, when a contractor or businessman has to pay bribes to public officials in order to be awarded a public contract, he or she tries to compensate for his losses through several methods. The rights of the public are safeguarded by God. Neither Islamic law nor modern legal systems tolerate breaches of these rights. If something is stolen from public funds, you cannot justify it by referring to the principles set forth in the *Mecelle* (a 19th-century codification of Islamic law by Ahmet Cevdet Paşa) or by indulging in demagoguery. You may set off by giving messages about Islamic principles about honesty and righteousness, but you may find yourselves deep down a dark alley. In such a case, those who invest their hopes in you will suffer from a great disappointment.

I would like to briefly add here the following: We should treat people with compassion. Our Prophet said, "Help your brother, whether he is an oppressor or he is an oppressed one." To which the Companions replied, "O Messenger of God! It is all right to help him if he is oppressed, but how should we help him if he is an oppressor?" "By preventing him from oppressing others," replied the Prophet. The noble Prophet advises us to stand against oppression, assault and murder. By explaining the evil character of these acts, people should be discouraged from committing them. When we opt to do this, this will bring about mutual affection and union, not division or conflict.

I had expected the people to be able to say amen to my supplications

A certain segment of the media have made much ado about it, distorting the facts. People were deceived with the lie, "He cursed us." Did you really curse them?

They persistently maintained the misunderstanding. Let me explain with an example. If a person repeatedly attacks you with lies and notoriety, you lose your patience at some point, and say, "If I am as you describe me, then may God curse me; but if I am not, then may God curse you for these lies and slander." This was the supplication I made at that time. I did not name any person, party or group specifically. I only described certain attributes and acts. "Whoever does this or that," I said. If they don't bear those attributes or if they haven't committed those acts, why do they take the curse personally? I would expect those who voice that slander based on some conspiracies or illusions in newspapers to say "amen" to my supplication. But they couldn't. On the contrary, they opted to abuse it. I am still of the same position. If we are a gang or organization or "parallel" state, then may God curse us; but if not, may He curse those who attribute this slander to this innocent movement! Those who cannot say "amen" to this supplication with an easy conscience should be concerned over their fate.

At least leave the prep schools not affiliated with us alone

Deputy Prime Minister and government spokesperson Bülent Arınç has claimed that some people had threatened the prime minister with regard to the government's plan to shut down prep schools. He said, "They said, 'Abandon this plan or we will overthrow your government.' And I rose to the challenge. I told them, 'Do whatever you plan to do; we will not retreat'." Can you comment on this claim?

First and foremost: Whoever makes this claim must prove it and take the matter to court. A public announcement should also be made, naming the people who made that threat. Blackmailing the government is a grave offense. If this claim was made in connection with groundless suspicions, I see no need to comment on it.

As you know, the plan to shut down the prep schools is not a novel development. Indeed, at that time, the names of former education ministers were mentioned and it was said that they failed to implement that plan, and the current minister was named as the person who would implement it. It follows that this plan had long been on the agenda and, perhaps, a promise was made concerning its implementation. There were press reports that such a promise had been made and that records of it can be found in the state's cosmic rooms (chambers where top secret documents are held). It has now become crystal clear that the plan to close the prep schools is not justified in terms of improvements to the education system. The obvious intention is to block the Hizmet Movement's educational activities. "Do not send your children to their schools and prep schools," we can hear being said at the election rallies of the ruling party. In other words, the government's intention is to start with the prep schools and proceed with the schools. Then they will try to ensure that the Hizmet Movement's schools abroad are shut down. In this context, Nazlı Ilıcak's analysis seems to be a very plausible explanation. She suggests that the government might have received prior intelligence about the graft investigations, and with the assumption that we could prevent them, it wanted to use the prep schools plan as blackmail or as a psychological operation or a (way to) shelter (itself).

I'm having a hard time understanding how they can this easily risk the unity and integrity of the entire country over nothing

Here, I should note that it would have been better if they had made their intention public, saying, for example, "We don't want the Hizmet Movement to engage in the prep schools business." They shouldn't have victimized the prep schools which are not affiliated with the Hizmet Movement. It is sad to see that many people who had labored hard to run prep schools will be unfairly treated in this process. It has been said that 3,000 of the 3,800 prep schools are not affiliated with the Hizmet Movement. If they had publicly told us, we would have said: "OK. If this is a life and death matter for you, we will ask our colleagues to shut down their prep schools in within a specified timeframe." This way innocent people would not be victimized in the process.

On a different note, I would like to say the following: The Ministry of Education, and even the government, should concentrate on more serious problems. Currently, social crises and cultural erosion entrap individuals and families. I recently read about it in an academic article. If I remember correctly, the number of suicides rose by 36 percent in 12 years. Likewise, drug abuse is widespread at high schools and 32 percent of students drink alcohol. One psychiatrist says the number of those receiving treatment for drug abuse rose 17-fold in 10 years. These figures are frightening in that they threaten society's moral and other values.

Given the fact that such huge problems pose great risks for the education system and even the country's future, how can the plan to shut down prep schools be justified as an effort to save the education system? Will this decay be prevented by closing down the prep schools? As far as I know, the schools and prep schools affiliated with the Hizmet Movement try to combat this decay. I am particularly concerned about the potential vacuum that will emerge in the Southeast. I have a hard time understanding how it is that those running the country can so comfortably put the country's unity and integrity at risk just to pursue their small interests.

I am also a victim; whoever is involved in illegal wiretapping should face justice

A large number of sound recordings (of phone conversations) have been leaked. Some circles in particular accuse the Hizmet Movement of leaking these tapes.

Similar accusations had been made in the past. However, those who direct these accusations have not so far presented evidence. Given that no strong or convincing evidence is being presented on such a critical and delicate issue, it is fair to believe that the accusers have something different in mind.

Everyone is talking on this matter. It is a complicated issue. There are legally wiretaps carried out upon a court order. But there are also illegal wiretaps. No matter what, those who relied on illegal methods to listen in on phone calls should be identified and brought to justice. This should be done regardless of the perpetrator's identity and affiliation. My friends and I are also victims of illegal wiretapping. Black propaganda methods have been used to undermine our image; we are openly targeted and accused in the media. We can deal with this by relying on legal options only. If someone relied on irregular and illegal methods to wiretap, they should be brought to justice. But I should also note that those who accuse a large movement of the illegal wiretappings despite having no evidence for their accusation should also answer before the law. The judiciary should question them as to how they make these accusations. It is impossible to deal with illegality by relying on illegal means. I believe complaining about the sound recordings but also using some of them as part of election campaigning is not reconcilable with ethical and legal principles.

PART 3

We are not and will not be a political party.
Therefore, we are not a rival of any political
party. We stand at an equal distance to everyone.
Nevertheless, we make public our hopes and
concerns about the future of our country.

This is not about a fight between Hizmet and the government. The matter at hand is the weakening of rights and freedoms

O n the surface, it appears that there is a row between the government and the Hizmet Movement. Articles were written to analyze this row. Some say, "We can change a party we don't like through elections, but how can we change a community we don't like?" What do you think about this?

I must note first of all that this is not a row between the AK Party and the Hizmet Movement. There has been a serious regression in fundamental rights and freedoms over the last few years. The offensive and subversive language utilized by politicians is making every social segment into "the other" and polarizing society. During the Gezi Park protests, I raised my objection to the description of protesters as *çapulcu* (bandits). This also applies for the Alevis. Turkey has failed to introduce democratic solutions for their most fundamental rights. Perhaps there is a deliberate procrastination in this regard. We supported a project to build a joint mosque-cemevi complex but received unexpectedly harsh reactions.

Second, we are not and will not be a political party. Therefore, we are not a rival of any political party. We stand at an equal distance to everyone. Nevertheless, we make public our hopes and concerns about the future of our country. I think this is one of our most natural and democratic rights. I don't understand why some people do not like us enjoying this democratic right of ours. Telling the people at the helm of the country "I have such and such ideas" should not be a crime. In advanced democracies, individuals and civil society organizations freely disseminate their views and criticisms about the country's political issues, and no one expresses any concern about this.

I must add that every institution established and run by our companions are open to public scrutiny and operate in full compliance with the law. In other words, there is a completely transparent structure in place. The recent developments have shown clearly who is not transparent. Participation in the Hizmet Movement is voluntary. It is regrettable to see volunteers of the Hizmet Movement depicted as members of a clandestine organization despite the fact that these people exhibit full compliance with the law. There are public servants from diverse ideological groups in every public institution. A public servant may be right-ist, leftist, Alevi, Sunni, non-Muslim, a Kurd, a Turk, what have you, but he or she is supposed to perform their duties properly. What matters is their compliance with the laws and regulations when performing their duties. If public servants are profiled or face unfounded charg-es, this is a breach of their fundamental rights and free-doms. If you talk about an imagined "parallel struc-ture" out of the blue, then your illusions will create thousands of such structures for you. And you end up with oppression against those people.

Partisanship is one thing, supporting democratic developments another

Why do you now oppose a political party you have sup-ported over the last 12 years? Were your interests aligned and reconciled before?

We have never established cooperation based on the recognition of interests with anybody. We have abstained from doing this because this is the lesson we draw from the Qur'an and the Sunnah. I have always seen the pursuit of strong and influential positions as a betrayal of our values. I would never say anything about choices other people make. But I have always viewed the pursuit of worldly and material gains as detrimental to my afterlife. This is also the case with my friends. We have never asked for a position such as general manager, governor, district governor or minister. If someone has done so in the past—and I do not remember such a thing happening—they are no longer linked to us. I have forwarded this sentiment of mine to state officials.

We have tried to extend support on such issues as the improvement of democracy and fundamental rights and freedoms. We would support any party to make sure anti-democratic practices come to an end and that the culture of a pluralistic democracy would become permanent. Unconditional partisanship is one thing, and lending support to democratic practices is another.

We now stand where we were before. We should look at who is moving away from this standpoint. A political party which has up until recently taken steps to expand the sphere of fundamental rights and freedoms is now considering censoring the Internet and introducing bills that would make this country an intelligence state. Is it possible to think of us as supporting attempts to do harm to social cohesion through strong and insulting discourse and to shelve democratic customs? If the whole issue is restricted to the Hizmet Movement, you may try tolerating the repressive measures. However, the ongoing developments should be analyzed from a broader perspective. Unfortunately, Turkey is being alienated from the world. A Turkey which becomes isolated on the global stage and loses its democratic richness will hurt not only the people in this country but also everyone who takes Turkey as a model for themselves.

In the fourth part of this series, to be published tomorrow, Gülen talks about his support for the settlement process and laments the government's belated steps to resolve the Kurdish issue.

Did the people we worked with together for 12 years turn bad after the corruption investigation?

The Hizmet Movement is being accused of being a gang or (terrorist) organization. There are even rumors that it will face a crackdown after the (local) elections (on March 30).

Unfortunately, many things are being said out of anger. I think every insult imaginable has already been made. They have consumed many things. Meanwhile, totally unfair accusations have been voiced. Following the campaign to toss around such labels as "(terrorist) organization," and "gang," efforts are also being made to influence the judiciary. It is now clear that, as has been said in election rallies, a lawsuit will be launched. If no crime can be found despite searching hard for it, it hurts the sense of justice to push laws beyond their limits to invent one, doesn't it?

The concept and ambiguous accusation of the existence of a "parallel structure" applies to virtually every segment of society. That is, there is no end to inventing offenses based on beliefs, ideologies, communal identities or parties of the people who work in public institutions. Today, you may declare a specific community as a "parallel" structure or as a "gang." In the future, others may claim the same for other communities. Thus, any person who works for the state and is sympathetic to any social, political or religious community may be accused of membership in a "parallel state." What is more, no one can guarantee that those who parrot today these accusations of a "parallel state" will not face the same accusations in the future. The practice of creating suspicions about certain people or groups with such unfounded accusations destroys the very sense of fairness, justice and order.

If a public servant does not comply with the orders of his or her superiors, there are laws that set forth the sentences for this offense. His or her noncompliance is punished under the law. Yet if the matter is taken outside the legal course and thousands of people are labeled and reshuffled unlawfully, this oppression cannot be explained or justified in either this world or the next (i.e., on the Day of Judgment).

To force the judicial authorities to invent crimes and launch lawsuits against these people would be amplified oppression and the general public will find it unacceptable. Moreover, sham trials will not be successful. Moreover, if you call these people, who make total compliance with the law their lifestyle, a network, then people will ask: You have been working with these people for 12 years and they were good people during that time, but suddenly, after the launch of the graft and bribery investigation, you realized that they are evil. Is that so? We must never forget the verse recited in every Friday sermon: "God commands you to act with fairness." That is, He orders us not to breach the rights of others.

To supporters they say "We made the soldiers kneel down," but to the army officers they say "It wasn't us, it was Hizmet"

For a long time, government sources have been attributing all adverse things at home and abroad to the Hizmet Movement, and all good, democratic and favorable things to themselves. Now, with the defendants in the Ergenekon trial being released, they are resorting to the same method in an effort to leave the Hizmet Movement with the bill. And occasionally this propaganda works. What do you say about this?

They tried to delude many social segments with this slander. For instance, they told some media groups, "We have no problem with you, but the Hizmet Movement is messing with you." Today, we understand from the voice recordings posted on the Internet that the officials who govern the country abandoned their proper duties and worked hard to ensure that these people were sentenced. They directly meddled in public tenders to push the businessmen who were deservedly awarded the contracts out. What is tragic here is that they commit grave sins by putting the blame of these errors on innocent people. Gossiping, backbiting, slander and aspersions abound, and one cannot help but feel sorry about it.

The saddest part is about the military. Those who boasted, behind closed doors, about "making the military submit to civilians" or "putting an end to military tutelage" told the military authorities, "We would iron out this problem, but the Hizmet Movement is preventing us." And yet they (the government) quickly passed a bill specifically for MİT Undersecretary Hakan Fidan. Had they really wanted and had they been sincere, they could have enacted a bill to save former Chief of General Staff Gen. İlker Başbuğ and other senior military officers overnight.

Moreover, I would like to convey to you a feeling of mine. My friends have witnessed numerous times my eyes fill with tears, seeing how those retired military officers were detained. "If only the people who wear this honorable uniform had not been faced with this situation," I had said. But I am in no position to meddle with the laws in force or make any suggestion in this context. A coup is a serious accusation and judicial authorities are supposed to, in accordance with the rules that govern them, hold those responsible accountable. But perhaps a legal remedy could have been found while taking into consideration the ages or medical condition of those people advanced in age and used to being treated with respect all their lives.

This is how I feel. It has always been so. It really runs counter to the facts to say that it is the Hizmet Movement that put them in that position. A senior retired police intelligence official recently gave an interview to a journalist. My friends read it to me from the Internet. "We informed Mr. Prime Minister before every operation we conducted," he had said. This statement, mentioned in a column, was not denied by the government. Now we have the right to ask: If the government knew of all operations beforehand, isn't it a great sin to talk about a conspiracy and raise suspicions about certain groups? If there really was a conspiracy, why didn't you take action to deal with it in a timely manner? If you knew, but failed to take action to prevent it, then wouldn't this make you an accomplice to the conspiracy?

Part 4

The people voiced democratic demands and, initially, there were innocent protests. These protests could have been tolerated. Officials could have visited the protesters and learned about their demands. Instead, the protests were violently suppressed. Is the shopping center that was to be built there worth a single drop of blood (shed during the protests)?

He could have approached the Gezi protests with tolerance, listened to grievances

Is a shopping center worth spilling blood over? Is it worth taking a life?

During the Ambassadors' Conference in Ankara, ambassadors were told to "explain well this organization" at their posts abroad. In a sense, Turkish ambassadors were ordered to denounce the Turkish schools abroad. Can you comment on this order?

When I hear news about Turkish officials' efforts to undermine the Turkish schools abroad, my heart aches and I seek refuge in God. Unfortunately, this appetite for destruction pushes all fair limits. These schools were established through the great self-sacrifice of the people of Anatolia. Almost everyone in Turkey has seen these schools, be they rightists, leftists, neo-nationalists, the religious or atheists, officials from the AK Party, the (main opposition) Republican People's Party (CHP), the Nationalist Movement Party (MHP), the Grand Unity Party (BBP), the Felicity Party (SP), the Peace and Democracy Party (BDP)—people from all walks of life. I have not heard even one person say, "These schools are harmful, and they should be shut down." No rational or political argument or criterion can be employed to advocate the closure of these schools.

Our friends who established these schools faced numerous material and immaterial hardships. They brought the embracing nature of the people of Anatolia to these countries. With them, they brought the Anatolian people's tolerance. They took our universal values with them. To turn a blind eye to the activities of these people who introduce our culture and language to all the countries of the world is ingratitude. You cannot conceal this manifest truth. Whatever they do, this wise society sees and knows everything. Therefore, their failure to prevent these activities or undermine these schools may lead them to delirium. They are struggling uncontrollably. This also needs to be known.

God willing, the caravan will go on

Turkey cannot emerge as a strong international player in the globalizing world if you fail to ensure that volunteer organizations and lobbies support Turkey in the international arena. Turkey cannot survive if it isolates itself from the external world. In this day and age, this applies not only to Turkey but to every other country as well. Turkey needs the support of the people who nurture love and sympathy for it everywhere around the world. Societies need to know more about and understand each other for global peace.

I feel much pain in seeing how these charity activities are being sabotaged and misrepresented in the eyes of foreign people. Despite this, we will try to maintain our respect and politeness toward everyone. This is what we have always done and will always do as this is what our character tells us to do.

In this transient world, we will speak ill of no one; we will not break anyone's heart; we will continue to promote good and amiable relations with everyone. Our actions will be guided by the following words of Bediüzzaman Said Nursi: "I forgive everyone who caused me hardship and anguish, the torture I was subjected to, and the ordeals I went through for many years. I have known nothing of worldly pleasure in my life of over 80 years. I have spent all my life on the battleground, in dungeons or in prison. I was barred from communication for months. I was treated like a criminal at war tribunals. I forgive those who oppressed me, those who sent me into exile many times, those who sought to put me in prison on trumped-up charges, and those who paved the way for my imprisonment."

True, as a believer, I promised to share these feelings. I will not be angry with anyone. I promised to welcome death smiling and treat divine hardship and bliss as the same.

Our friends should not despair. With God's grace and permission, this service done for this nation, for the future of this nation and for all of humanity will continue. Thanks to God's favor and generosity, neither slander nor ill-intentioned campaigns can halt this bandwagon of service. People with a pure conscience and mind will soon uncover this slander and these lies.

As I noted elsewhere, there may be certain fanatical efforts to block our path, but as long as there are souls who are open to dialogue, tender people who smile at everyone, conscientious people who are aware of their sins, souls who regret their wrong or misguided deeds, and wise people who seek to build their future on reasonableness, we will mend our shattered souls and recover ourselves and continue to love everyone anew. This is what we should do with respect to the recent developments.

Unfortunately, during the Gezi protests...

On the other hand, I believe it is extremely dangerous to polarize society along various lines or identities in Turkey. This is akin to playing with fire. How can a parent incite some members of the family against other members of the same family who hold different ideologies? We are a large family with roots dating back several centuries. We must refrain from treating our differing ideologies and diverse identities as reasons to quarrel or engage in conflict. Everyone must respect diversity. Freedom of speech and expression cannot be restricted. While the views of the majority certainly deserve respect, the views of minority groups should be treated with the same level of respect as well. If you suppress the masses, this will cause friction along social fault lines. And this is such a big risk that no political party can take for whatever political gain.

Unfortunately, this is what happened during the Gezi Park protests. The people voiced democratic demands and, initially, there were innocent protests. These protests could have been tolerated. Officials could have visited the protesters and learned about their demands. Instead, the protests were violently suppressed. Is the shopping center that was to be built there worth a single drop of blood (shed during the protests)? Is it worth a single human life? Naturally, pressure led to violence and a local issue turned into a national security issue. And the evil networks which were waiting for an opportunity to stir up chaos stepped onto the stage, and we were very concerned at that time. Our friends all around the world prayed for peace. They prayed the Prayer of Need. And yet it was said that these protests were somehow masterminded by the Hizmet Movement. May God endow them with understanding.

Peace and settlement process must continue, must include entire Southeast

What do you think about the settlement process and its current state?

This is something I had spoken about previously on a number of occasions. A believer always favors peace. A believer adopts the attitude required for peace. There are problems that have accumulated over time. In the past, violence was wielded to solve these problems. But this did not settle it; it only exacerbated it further. Now there is a process of peace and reconciliation. This shouldn't be disrupted. This is a good opportunity for both sides to forget about hostilities and turn back from their mistakes.

A state must be fair in its dealings with its citizens. Fundamental rights and freedoms should not be seen or used as a card in bargaining.

Even before the settlement process began, I had expressed my perspective about education in one's mother tongue. But no step was taken to this end. This matter is still in abeyance. At once we must raise teachers who are capable of teaching in Kurdish. This is not something that can be done upon demands from the public. The state must take the first step. In taking this step, we must refrain from words, attitudes and behavior that may give the impression that we are doing this as a favor. The region was home to numerous major civilizations and intellectuals. In addition to recognizing the due rights and freedoms of its Kurdish citizens, Turkey must extend a helping hand to the Kurds in other regions. We must re-establish and reinforce our cultural and historical ties with them.

We have three fundamental problems: These were outlined by Bediüzzaman almost a century ago as ignorance, poverty and disunity. These problems have bred despair, deception, circumvention, mutual distrust, and so on.

Political, non-political—everyone in one place

We need to discuss these problems on a common platform. This is not something that can be done with disdain and arrogance. If conciliation is to be achieved, this would be all-inclusive, embracing the entirety of the region and diverse groups. No one should be excluded from it. Common denominators should be found to embrace political and non-political groups. We should let local people solve their problems with their own capabilities. If quick steps are not taken in this regard, I fear the settlement process may come to a halt. Fine, let us focus on stopping the bloodshed. Even this indicates a certain level of pragmatism. But we should have targets beyond that point. We must create an atmosphere in which everyone—Turks, Kurds, Sunnis, Alevis, Arabs, Syriacs, and so on—can co-exist as members of the same family in happiness and prosperity.

If you're going to look for a 'supreme mastermind,' look for it in the grace of God

Some circles recently used the term "supreme mastermind" to tarnish the image of the Hizmet Movement and imply that the movement is supported by external actors.

Making this accusation is a grave sin. I suppose people have never been insulted or encountered such extensive lies and slanderous remarks before. If there is something they are aware of, they should inform the public about it; otherwise, they are denigrating Muslims. The smear campaign is so unbearable that we are witnessing new lies and even slander every day. The desire for prosperity makes hearts insensitive; and in that case, you cannot feel properly. You ignore spirituality; you even humiliate it. When the heart becomes insensitive and attaches great importance to the world through the desire for prosperity, you'll suppose that it is all about this world. And then you simply do not worry about committing sins. The Qur'an recommends sensitivity and emotion in the heart. When the hardness of the heart takes the soul hostage, one can resort to every method to attain his goals irrespective of whether they are legitimate or not. Sadly, one of the reasons for the current stalemate is hardness in the hearts. But if they are looking for a mastermind of the Hizmet Movement, I would say it is the solidarity and protection that God bestows on consultation and brotherhood.

The Hizmet Movement does not depend on any fading and mortal power or actor; it has made advances because God has been graceful; as long as He protects, no one will ever hurt it. Muslims are supposed to act with caution. They do not backbite about their brothers and sisters based on false reports. Unfortunately, there is no room for the afterlife in the agendas of those who express their desires for worldly possessions all the time. This may drive the people towards social deviation and religious distortion. Many unusual statements that contradict with religious belief have been made. Media outlets covered them extensively. These are contradictory to religious norms; but even those who are supposed to remain silent are talking. We can save our souls from the disorder and corruption surrounding us by renewing our thoughts and emotions on a daily basis. Hearts are hardened if theoretical Islam turns into a lifestyle and, in that case, one forgets about his own responsibility and slanders Muslims all the time. Things will settle down eventually. People in this country will look at each other's face again. People who turn in the same direction (i.e., towards Mecca) while performing their prayers should avoid making strong remarks that they would feel ashamed of in the future.

PART 5

_____

*People and the authorities know and have
observed my acts and words for the last 50 years.
Is it possible for a person who has a secret
agenda to conceal this agenda for 50 years?*

Each party has respected candidates

I see saying one has to vote for this party or that as a form of pressure on one's conscience

Only days are left until the elections. There are debates on what party the movement will support.

I cannot see it as proper for Muslims to talk about this all the time and think that the ballot box is the real meaning of life. Of course the ballot box holds a crucial importance for the future of this country; but it is not everything. It is impossible not to become upset realizing that focusing on the ballot box only makes some people comfortable in telling lies. As for the debate on who we should vote for, I have always asked my friends to cast their votes based on their personal conviction. I believe that asking them to vote for a certain party is a type of pressure; in addition, I also consider engagement with a certain party isolation from other segments of society. Our clear and plain stance in the referendum was not for a certain party; it was for the introduction of democratic steps. It appears that this stance is not being appreciated.

There is now a party chairman who constantly throws around insults. And, unfortunately, the wise men of that party prefer deep silence. With the exception of strong partisans, I have frequently noticed that the AK Party support base is upset with this. If a person internalizes and acknowledges such grave accusations and insults, he or she may still vote for that party; but I believe that these remarks which would be hurtful to anybody have also been hurtful to our friends. Everyone will consider their own situation and analyze the mayoral candidates. In the end, this is not a general election. The candidates are more important than the parties; there are many valuable candidates in all parties. Whatever party you vote for, you will not have committed a sin.

Speculations abound regarding your stay in the US and about whether you will return to Turkey. Can you comment on this matter?

I wanted to think well of those who had asked me to return. Similar calls had previously been made. Regarding these calls, I could sense the real intention. But I continue to stick to courtesy and a positive attitude toward believers. First and foremost, I am just a believer among many believers. I have always kept my feet on the ground. This is the way I have lived my life. In my opinion, the highest station one can attain is to be a true servant of God. It is my wish to die in this station. I have no connection or ties to any external power, force or group. Such a thing is out of question. Those caught in the web of external powers, forces or groups are those who run after prosperity, power and other worldly stations or posts. Unfortunately, those who aspire to seize power despotically upon growing stronger and to never abandon it start to see as a danger those who don't nurture aspirations for power and who even specifically refrain from such pursuits with a focus on how to attain God's contentment and His bliss in the Hereafter. They try to portray these people as a threat to the state, but they essentially perceive them as a threat to their plans.

Even in the most underdeveloped societies, people are tried for their words and acts and verdicts are passed about them based on what they say or do. People and authorities know and have observed my acts and words for the last 50 years. Is it possible for a person who has a secret agenda to conceal this agenda for 50 years?

I will decide about whether or not to return to Turkey not based on the convictions of some people but after consulting with friends whose intentions I find considerably sincere. As I said before, if I return, I will return not as someone else but as I am—as the son of Ramiz Efendi who served as the imam of the Üç Şerefeli Cami (mosque).

Calamities come and go; don't be grieved

You have for some time now stopped delivering sermons over the Internet. Those affiliated with the movement wonder about your sentiments under such strong pressure and insults. Is there anything you would like to tell them?

We have to remain patient in the face of what is happening to us. We should never abandon our lenient and decent style. People have suffered from different problems in different periods. Important figures such as Imam Rabbani, Hasan al-Shadhili and Mawlana Khalid al-Baghdadi have suffered. The brutality and persecution Bediüzzaman was subjected to should be remembered. He was subjected to all sorts of brutality. We are not comparable to these remarkable people. But if this is their case and this is their method, then we need to be willing to take all sorts of sufferings. We should not resent. We need to pray to God all the time and tell Him, "We are content with God as our Lord, and with Islam as our religion, and with Muhammad, peace and blessings be upon him, as our Prophet." We should never feel offended by the way He treats us. We should always be content with Him.

Troubles are temporary. If our communication and relationship with God is perfect, we will secure our afterlife even when we experience huge troubles. If they do not seek worldly advantages and assets, those who dedicate themselves to this cause will have eternal gains in the afterlife. Everybody should stay where they are. Depending on the circumstances and the conjuncture, different options should be tried to reach the destination even if they block the main road and options. That destination is universal human values. These people I referred to above were never pessimistic; so we should be like them. We should keep our hopes high. "Hopelessness is such a quagmire that if you fall into it, you will drown; but if you grab on to your resolution, you will be saved." This is what Mehmet Akif (a renowned Turkish poet) says about hopelessness. We believe that this bleak weather and climate will eventually disappear. We have always held this hope.

You also referred to what I have been subjected to so far. I did not complete my military service when the May 27 (1960) coup was staged. I was persecuted then. I was persecuted in the March 12 (1971) coup. I had to run away like a bandit for six years during the Sept. 12 (1980) coup. Former President Turgut Özal exerted his authority at a time when he was feeling strong; so they left me alone. But this was not the end. I traveled to Mecca to perform the Hajj. Things were unpleasant for me once again. I gave a statement at a state security court. The legal case Prosecutor Nuh Mete Yüksel filed in the aftermath of Feb. 28 (the 1997 coup) lasted for years. Despite the denigration I was subjected to in that case, the chief prosecutor here in New Jersey showed me respect. He welcomed me at the door (to the building). He helped me to the (witness) chair himself so that I could sit down. He then washed his own glass, filled it with water and offered it to me, telling me that my mouth may go dry given that I was testifying. I experienced this here. He did not know me at all. Then we discussed as to whether we should send him a gift for this gentle treatment. When I presented him a gift, he said he could not accept a gift from a person whose legal case he had handled. I said to myself that these people still survive despite all negative developments thanks to this legal philosophy. Because of this legal understanding, they still play an influential role in world politics.

I should also tell you that I was imprisoned during my military service because I was delivering sermons. A commander who was protecting me allowed me to deliver sermons, which he also attended. As he was preparing to leave our unit, he hugged me in tears and said I would face repression after he goes. And what he said came to be. They sent me to prison. I have also been subjected to different types of persecution and repression at different times. However, the things I am experiencing now are not comparable to what I experienced in the past. The lies, insults and denigrating remarks... But everyone reflects their own character in their attitudes and remarks. In the end, we cannot say anything to anybody.

A new constitution needed to exit from turmoil

Turkey is going through hard times. Sometimes people become pessimistic because of the ongoing turmoil. How, in your opinion, can Turkey get out of this atmosphere?

Above all, I should stress that in such times it is strongly necessary to pray to God and seek refuge in His mercy. We should be worried about the fate of those who are not worried about their fate. Those who feel content all the time and hold doubts about the faith of others will face a great danger from the religious perspective. 'Umar (the second caliph) was concerned about his fate (despite being one of the 10 people who have been promised Paradise). And so we should be worried about our fate. We need to seek refuge in His mercy and protection. We need to say, "O God, hold my hand. For if You do not, I will be doomed." Like individuals, faith and submission are sanctuaries for communities as well. Those who do not seek refuge in this sanctuary may be crushed under their ego. May God protect us from this.

This is one side of the coin. The other side is as follows: In order to overcome the current turmoil, this country needs a new climate. A new constitution is a must to guarantee fundamental rights and freedoms. I believe there should be growing popular demand and pressure on the relevant figures and institutions so that they will make a democratic constitution based on the recognition of universal legal principles. Many intellectuals offer similar analyses. A Turkey which moves away from its own values and people will also move away from the world.

Today, individuals and societies have greater importance than their states. It is impossible to implement a project that is imposed on the people. At the beginning of this century, Bediüzzaman said predominance over the civilized is possible through persuasion, not coercion. Therefore, repression of people will not remain the same all the time. They cannot be permanent. We have to approach the events and developments via patience, prudence and caution. If you approach the developments via the patience and submission they deserve and deal with them as such, reason will dominate eventually. And when this happens, those who had engaged in sin before will feel embarrassed; and you open up your hearts noting that this is not a day of condemnation and making sure that they do not feel this way. This has been the case throughout history. If you are traveling in the opposite direction when people are moving away from you; the distance between you becomes larger. And the day you need union and cooperation you will realize that you have made a mistake. You realize this but it is too late. We need to think about nothing but committing ourselves to our service and duties. This is my humble opinion on this matter.

HOW THE INTERVIEW
WAS COVERED

Gülen's messages emerge as a glimmer of hope for Turkey

I n his interview, Fethullah Gülen touched on a number of matters, including limitations on rights and freedoms and the futility of efforts to cover up allegations of corruption. Intellectuals, opinion leaders, politicians and many other people from all walks of life noted that the interview consisted of information and assessments by a scholar or intellectual who is victimized and who exhibits his belief in the rule of law and democracy. Mr. Gülen's interview concerning the hardship-laden process Turkey faced attracted a great deal of interest among the public. In the interview, published in a five-part series in the *Zaman* daily, Mr. Gülen responded to the slander he and the Hizmet Movement faced and called on everyone to act in moderation. Figures from all segments of society lent support to Mr. Gülen's commonsense remarks. These views can be summed up as follows:

Yılma Durak, a well-respected figure among nationalists in Eastern Turkey: Gülen spoke about

Turkey's problems in the interview in a very polite way. Everyone can benefit from his remarks. Unfortunately, we have witnessed a wrong attitude exhibited against Gülen. Unfortunately, the prime minister wants to hush up corruption and theft by defaming Gülen. This is not correct. We are simple Muslims and such things make us sad. All these attacks against Gülen will backfire and those who attack him will hurt themselves. They are talking about a so-called "parallel state." Fear God! They fling mud at him so that he suffers from the lingering effects of the defamation. This does not befit the prime minister. There are efforts to legitimize theft. Isn't theft a cardinal sin? You are violating the rights of orphans. Fear God!

Former Culture and Tourism Minister Ertuğrul Günay: I closely followed Fethullah Gülen's statements. Since the beginning, Gülen contributed to broadcasting the truth to a wider audience with his usual softer-toned remarks. The prime minister has been hurling unfair accusations at Mr. Gülen and the Hizmet Movement, which seeks to raise a generation of well-educated people. Despite this, Mr. Gülen adopted a cautious style that avoids polemics and explained his position and perspective to everyone. I hope Mr. Gülen's patience is shared by everyone and that these dark days are quickly replaced with hopeful and bright ones. I would like to thank him for his patience and moderation.

CEM Foundation President İzzettin Doğan: Mr. Fethullah Gülen gave convincing answers to accusations with a style befitting a religious scholar. The responsibility of proving the allegations lies primarily with the government. We see that Mr. Gülen's remarks about Alevis follow a style that befits him. Whatever Mr. Gülen said to me about Alevis for the last 15 years, I see he stood behind those words. Gülen proposed the construction of a mosque and a cemevi in the same complex 15 years ago. None of our Sunni sisters and brothers raised any objection to the construction of cemevis in Turkey. Our Sunni sisters and brothers made great contributions to the construction of many cemevis, and their support continues. Mr. Gülen's warning and assessments certainly paved the way for these good developments. I truly appreciated his remarks about social peace in Turkey.

Theologian Suat Yıldırım: Many wondered about what Mr. Gülen would say about the allegations which are being made public these days. This is why this interview was very relevant. First of all, Mr. Gülen starting his remarks with "I wouldn't expect" sums up his words. He did not expect these accusations and slander from the prime minister. He did not expect certain columnists to attack the Community although they had the opportunity to closely know and learn about this Community, which has been transparent for the last 50 years. He did not expect certain people, who were fair-minded friends, to be silent about the slander. There is no row between the Community and the Justice and Development Party (AK Party). However, a certain level of regression has recently been experienced regarding freedoms and rights. The alienation of certain social groups has emerged. We are not a political party, but we may voice our concerns about our country's future. This is not only our democratic right, it is also our democratic duty.

Prime Minister hurls insults while Gülen calls for moderation

Journalist/author Nazlı Ilıcak: I wrote the book *Her Taşın Altında "The Cemaat" mi Var?* (Is "The Movement" Behind Everything?) about the trial of certain military officers about one year ago. I argued in that book that there were efforts to hold the Community responsible for everything. These military officers produced fake evidence and held the Community responsible for it. Now the same is being done by those who were caught red-handed during the graft and bribery investigations. Mr. Gülen points at the same fact. I fully agree with him. First we need to find out if there is any corruption. You have indulged in corruption, but you bicker with Mr. Gülen. What can be his involvement here? I repeat, those who indulge in unlawfulness rush to use him as an excuse. Everyone is eager to accuse the Community of any adversity that may afflict them. This is a period of oppression. There has never been such an open tyrannical period since Feb. 28, 1997—when the Turkish military forced the coalition government led by the Welfare Party (RP) out of power, citing alleged rising religious fundamentalism in the country. It is shameful to voice such open and reckless accusations. This can't go on like this.

Journalist/author Lale Kemal: The prime minister continuously accuses the Community and outside circles. We witnessed how the graft and bribery operations were blocked by the government. The government targeted everyone, and in particular the Hizmet Movement, to do this. This is a problematic approach. We need to acknowledge that several good people or bureaucrats risked their career in an effort to prevent corruption. This is what Mr. Gülen draws attention to. We need to see that a few fair-minded men and women and thousands of people protesting anti-democratic practices may transform the society. There are slanders and insults against his personality and the movement inspired by his ideas. He properly responded to these in a calm manner. This is the first time that the

Turkish society is facing such grave insults by a prime minister. Mr. Gülen gave even-tempered responses to these insults, but they don't get the message. Mr. Gülen's words constitute a collective answer to the insults and attacks against his personality and the society. He responded in a reasonable and cool-headed manner.

He stresses peace and brotherhood

Felicity Party (SP) leader Mustafa Kamalak: Mr. Gülen spoke in a way that befits him. Peace or fraternity is what this country needs the most. May God be pleased with him; Mr. Gülen's messages always seek to achieve this peace. What caught my attention in this interview was this. "Being able to rule for a lifetime is not worth a single drop of blood," I had said, referring to the Gezi Park incidents. Mr. Gülen, too, asked, "Is a shopping center worth the life of a person?" This is the correct perspective. We used almost identical expressions.

Great service being carried out by Hizmet Movement, no one can deny this

Grand Unity Party (BBP) leader Mustafa Destici: The Hizmet Movement has been delivering great services for more than 40 years. This is done not only in Turkey but also in 160 countries around the world. The schools abroad are not referred to as the Community's schools or as Gülen schools. They are known as Turkish schools. These schools provide a good atmosphere for the improvement of economic and cultural ties as well. What the Hizmet Movement is doing is pretty obvious. It is trying to convey its values to various places around the globe without material expectations and it is making great contributions to world peace. With these services, it is extending a helping hand to the oppressed and disadvantaged states. I don't approve of the wording used against Mr. Gülen and I cannot understand how so many unfounded accusations may be hurled against him.

We find his views on expansion of liberties under Constitution important

Peace and Democracy Party (BDP) deputy Altan Tan: I closely followed Fethullah Gülen's interview. He made positive explanations about the agenda. In particular, his views that Kurds should settle their problems without intervention from outside and his emphasis on the education in one's mother tongue, and especially in Kurdish, are positive developments. I find his views about the need for drafting a constitution that would expand freedoms and liberties important.

Great gap exists between styles of Gülen and prime minister

Lawyer/columnist Orhan Kemal Cengiz: First of all, there is great gap in terms of wording, culture and manners. There is a sharp contrast between the harsh rhetoric employed by Erdoğan and what Gülen said in a mild-mannered and reconciliatory tone. It is refreshing for a cleric to emphasize democracy and rule of law in Turkey. Erdoğan has become a burden on the nation. Gülen is an actor in the new Turkey while Erdoğan speaks from the old Turkey. One represents what is new while the other what is old. Even a comparison of the wording reveals that Mr. Gülen largely talks about democracy and the rule of law. On the other hand, Erdoğan is obsessed with agents, traitors, spies, etc. This is the language of the 1930s. Mr. Gülen is speaking the language of 2014.

Highlights from the interview

Islamic scholar Fethullah Gülen, who has inspired a worldwide network active in education, charity and outreach, has described large-scale slander, pressure and oppression his Hizmet Movement faced as worse than that seen during anti-democratic military coup regimes witnessed by Turkey. He also called on his supporters to remain patient and steadfast and to not despair.

"What we are seeing today is 10 times worse than what we saw during the military coups," he said, adding to that "we face similar treatment (as seen during the military coups) but at the hands of civilians who we think follow the same faith as us."

Gülen's remarks represented a stark reminder of how he felt in comparison to past military coups, during which he said he was prosecuted and persecuted. His comparison confirmed what Turkish opposition parties were saying; namely, that the government in Turkey had staged a civilian coup and suspended the constitution and the rule of law in the country following the breakout of a corruption scandal on Dec. 17, 2013.

"But despite everything, I don't complain. ... All we can do is say 'This, too, shall pass,' and remain patient," Gülen added. He also predicted that the current oppression engaged in by the government will not last long. "Aggressors will be turned upside down when they least expect it," Gülen said.

Having stayed largely silent in the face of relentless attacks amounting to hate speech by beleaguered Prime Minister Recep Tayyip Erdoğan, who was incriminated in a massive corruption scandal, Gülen provided his account of how he saw the events in Turkey in the first interview with the Turkish media since Dec. 17.

Gülen explained his views on the corruption investigations, the March 30, 2013 local elections, whether he supports any political party, slander leveled against him, voice recordings that had been leaked to the Internet, the release of suspects in the Ergenekon trial, the settlement process with the country's Kurds, rumors on a possible lawsuit against members of the Hizmet Movement after the elections, Hizmet's alleged involvement in the takeover of the Fenerbahçe sports club, how he sees Turkey exiting from the crisis, his return to Turkey and other questions many had been wondering about.

Gülen makes it clear that no conspiracy, slander and smear attacks can overcome truth, prudence and foresight. "What evidence are they relying on when speaking so confidently? I really don't know," he said, challenging those who spread lies about the Hizmet Movement to bring forth evidence in support of their allegations. Recalling that believers have been denigrated throughout history, Gülen emphasized that "everyone acts in accordance with their character."

Despite attacks and a campaign of defamation, Gülen said almost all of his friends have acted with fidelity. "There was virtually no shock or breakup from among our companions and friends," he noted in an apparent response to Erdoğan's failed efforts to drive a wedge between the leadership and the grassroots of the Hizmet Movement. Erdoğan repeatedly said there is a difference between the leaders of the Hizmet Movement and the members of the organization. "While the organization's members at the grassroots level are displaying sincerity, its leaders have taken a different position," Erdoğan noted, accusing the leadership of conspiring with what he called "international dark circles."

Recounting the Feb. 28, 1997 postmodern coup, during which he was victimized and forced to leave the country amid the military's ouster of an elected government, Gülen said he tried his best to prevent the coup from taking place, including appealing to political leaders to call for an early election to get a fresh mandate. "Tension was building and everyone was searching for ways to save the country from this predicament (the impending threat of a military coup) with minimal damage. And like many others, I said early elections might be the cure. I suggested early elections should be held under a new election law."

Gülen also talked about his alleged role in a conspiracy to change the management of the Fenerbahçe sports club, which boasts an estimated 25 million— some say over 30 million—supporters. However, a new voice recording leaked on YouTube early in March 2013 revealed that Prime Minister Erdoğan had attempted to get a candidate close to him elected as chairman of the Fenerbahçe sports club, instructing his son Bilal on how to prep his favored candidate with talking points.

"It has been understood that this claim (the Hizmet Movement taking over Fenerbahçe) has turned out to be an aspersion," Gülen said in reference to the voice recording. He added that "the emerging trend of our time is to attribute every inexplicable event to the Hizmet Movement and use it as a scapegoat." Gülen underlined that he rejoices the achievements of Turkish sport teams, be it Fenerbahçe, Galatasaray, Trabzon, Beşiktaş or any other team.

Gülen described remarks by Erdoğan's top advisor, Yalçın Akdoğan, as a trick. Akdoğan had suggested conspirators, a veiled reference to Hizmet, had used the Ergenekon and Sledgehammer coup plot trials, in which many military officials, including top brass, were convicted, to target the Turkish Armed Forces (TSK). They tried to blame Hizmet for what they had done, he said. Recalling that the government rushed a bill through Parliament to save one man, National Intelligence Organization (MİT) Undersecretary Hakan Fidan, from ongoing legal troubles in February 2012, Gülen said Erdoğan's government could have done the same for the others had it wanted.

Who is Fethullah Gülen?

Mr. Fethullah Gülen is a Turkish Muslim scholar, thinker, and poet, as well as an educational and humanitarian activist. He is regarded as the initiator and inspiration of the worldwide social movement known as Hizmet, which translates to service and is also known simply as the Gülen Movement. Gülen is noted for his pro-democracy, pro-science, pro-dialogue and anti-violence positions. In May 2008, Fethullah Gülen was listed as the most influential public intellectual in the world by Foreign Policy magazine. In 2013 he was named one of Time's 100 most influential people in the world.

Gülen's life and teachings exemplify values such as selfless service to one's community and to humanity in general, sincerity, as well as deep faith. As a testament to his humility, Gülen considers himself to be just one among the millions of volunteers in the social movement that he helped originate and which bears his name.

He denounces any attribution of leadership and instead spends most of his time reading, writing, and in worship. He is known for his deep respect for all creation, for his empathetic attitude, and his call to alleviate the suffering of humans in every corner of the world. The millions of volunteer participants in the Hizmet movement include students, academics, business owners, professionals, public officials, and farmers. The movement draws men and women, young and old, to contribute in multiple ways. Projects include tutoring centers, schools, colleges, hospitals, publishing houses and media outlets. In addition, the Hizmet movement operates a major relief organization named Kimse Yok Mu (KYM). The movement originated in Turkey, but now takes place in more than a hundred and fifty countries around the world.

Fethullah Gülen currently resides in Pennsylvania and continues to write and give talks on various important subjects related to spirituality and humanitarian service and causes.

Ekrem Dumanlı

Born in Yozgat, Turkey, in 1964, Ekrem Dumanlı graduated from the Department of Turkish Language and Literature at İstanbul University and worked for a time as a teacher of literature. In 1993, he started working as a reporter for the Culture and Art Desk of the *Zaman* daily newspaper. He was later assigned as Culture and Art Desk editor and publication coordinator. In 1997, Mr. Dumanlı went to the US to further his studies in the media, completing his Master's degree at Boston Emerson College. Returning to Turkey in 2001, Mr. Dumanlı was appointed editor-in-chief of Zaman. Still in this post, Mr. Dumanlı has written five books: *Kronik Gündemlere Pratik Çözümler* (Practical Solutions to Chronic Agenda Items), *28 Şubat Gölgesinde Amerika* (USA, Under the Shadow of Feb. 28), *Medya* (Media), *Haber Kılavuzu: Gazetecinin El Kitabı* (News Guide), and *Üç Mesele: İktidar, Medya, Ergenekon* (Three Issues: The Leading Power, Media, and Ergenekon). His articles have also been published by the foreign press, including "The Turkey-U.S. Divide" by the Los Angeles Times. A play he wrote, titled "The Last Trial," was performed on stage by the Istanbul World Stage Theatre. He has also been listed in Georgetown University's list of The 500 Most Influential Muslims in 2009.